WHAT IS
WAR?

Eduard Altarriba

Button
Books

"Dad, how do soldiers killing each other
solve the world's problems?"

Bill Watterson
*Calvin and Hobbes: Sunday
Pages 1985–1995*

Contents

Sometimes we meet people who see things very differently from us.
Then we can get angry and even argue because each person is convinced
that he or she is right and the other person is completely wrong.
It's these two clashing viewpoints that can lead to

• CONFLICT •

DIPLOMACY

POLITICS

When diplomacy and
politics fail to solve
conflicts, this can trigger
violence and

WAR

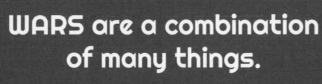

Some wars are between two countries fighting over where a border starts and ends.

Other times they are conflicts within a country, between different social, ethnic, or political groups.

Some wars have a long history that has been passed down from one generation to the next.

Conflicts don't usually have a single cause.

WARS are a combination of many things.

Sometimes a government goes to war to protect the interests of the country and its industry.

Sometimes a region wants to be independent, so it clashes with the rest of the country.

Sometimes, small, very powerful or very radical groups light the fuse that leads to conflict.

WHO IS WHO

The people involved in a war are all those individuals and organizations that, whether they like it or not, are part of an armed conflict.

NATIONAL ARMIES

There are around two hundred countries in the world and nearly all of them have an army even when not fighting a war.* States spend a large part of their money on maintaining an army. Every army has to respect the humanitarian laws signed by their government.

IRREGULAR FORCES

These are armed groups that do not belong to a national army. They are also called guerrillas, paramilitaries, insurgents, militias, or even terrorists. They can range from very small groups to very powerful armies with unofficial support from a particular government.

CIVILIAN POPULATION

Civilians are non-military people who might live in a war zone but don't fight. They are the main victims of a conflict. Despite international laws, they suffer violence, have problems getting food and other basic necessities, and often have to flee their homes.

*Andorra, Liechtenstein, and Samoa are among the few countries that have no army.

INTERNATIONAL ACTORS

These are foreign organizations or people that can have an influence on a conflict.

International organizations

The United Nations (UN) and the Red Cross are organizations that stand above states. Their role in conflicts is to monitor and take action to make sure human rights are respected.

NGOs

Non-governmental organizations (NGOs) do not belong to any government, so are generally neutral in a conflict. Their mission is to protect human rights and help victims.

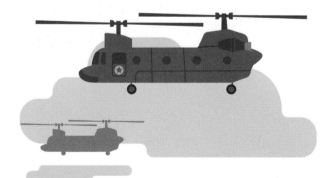

Foreign military intervention

Foreign governments may send military aid or troops to another country for humanitarian reasons or to protect their interests.

Public opinion

What the citizens of a foreign country think about a conflict is important, because it can encourage their government to intervene to help one side or another.

War is about
POWER

The winner of a war can put their friends or family members in government posts to rule over the people they have defeated, they can decide who collects taxes, they can keep their neighbors' goats or oil, and they can even write history as they see fit.

IT IS SAID THAT HISTORY IS WRITTEN BY THE VICTORS.

THAT'S WHY WE KNOW A LOT ABOUT THE ROMANS, BUT VERY LITTLE ABOUT THE GAULS, THE IBERIANS, AND THE OTHER PEOPLES THEY CONQUERED.

WE ALSO KNOW A LOT ABOUT KINGS AND GENERALS, BUT VERY LITTLE ABOUT THEIR SOLDIERS, AND EVEN LESS ABOUT ORDINARY WOMEN AND CHILDREN.

War is also a

BUSINESS

In a conflict, most people (including the victors) lose a lot, but a few people make a lot of money.

MERCENARIES

Mercenaries are professional soldiers who hire themselves out to anyone who will pay.

They have been around since ancient times, but now that countries have national armies they are less important than they once were.

ARMS MANUFACTURERS

These are companies involved in designing and producing all kinds of arms (weapons), from pistols to attack helicopters.

Every government in the world spends part of its resources on buying arms to maintain the military and technological power of its army.

ARMS DEALERS

According to international law, only states can buy weapons legally. This is why many irregular forces have to buy illegal weapons from arms dealers.

There are many illegal weapons in the world (especially small arms, such as guns). Smugglers also know ways to convert legal weapons into illegal ones.

CONTRACTORS

A war needs a lot of resources and there are always companies ready to provide them, from petrol for tanks to bank loans for buying weapons.

Companies are also needed once the war is over, to rebuild damaged infrastructure (bridges, roads, and buildings) and to pump in money to get the economy going again.

WEAPONS

Weapons of war are designed to wound and kill people. Over the centuries they have become increasingly good at their job: nowadays a well-equipped soldier has huge firepower and there are high-tech weapons with enormous destructive power.

CONVENTIONAL WEAPONS

▮LIGHT WEAPONS

These are weapons that can be carried by a single person.

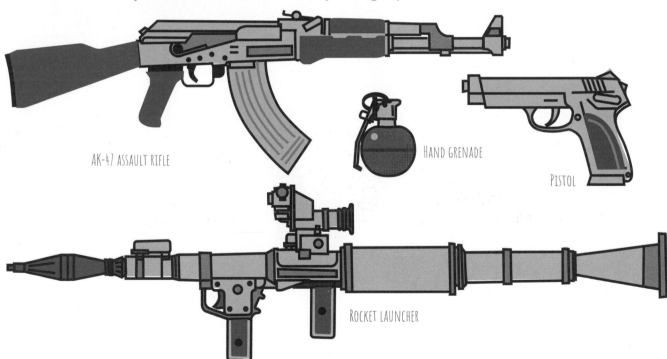

AK-47 ASSAULT RIFLE

HAND GRENADE

PISTOL

ROCKET LAUNCHER

Guns and anti-personnel landmines are the most common light weapons. They are also the easiest to sell illegally, and the ones that cause the most damage. It is estimated that 90 percent of casualties in conflicts are caused by these weapons.

ANTI-TANK LANDMINE

ANTI-PERSONNEL LANDMINE

◼ HEAVY WEAPONS

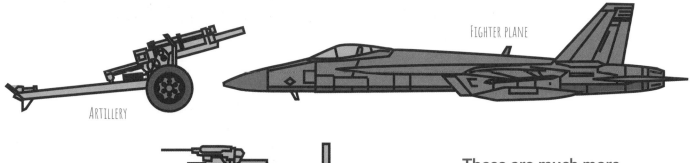

Fighter plane

Artillery

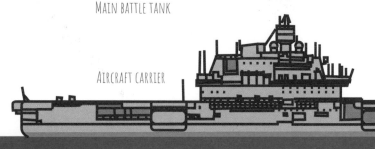

Main battle tank

These are much more sophisticated and expensive weapons. Only national armies have the money, soldiers, and military facilities that are needed to maintain a navy and an air force.

Aircraft carrier

NON-CONVENTIONAL WEAPONS

Nuclear

Nuclear weapons are based on atomic energy. Their destructive power is capable of wiping out an entire city. They also cause a cloud of radioactive contamination that affects people and the environment.

Biological

Biological weapons use bacteria, viruses, or toxins that can make people ill or harm the environment. They are banned under the 1993 Chemical Weapons Convention.

Chemical

Chemical weapons are made from toxic substances that can kill or cause serious harm to people. They are also banned under the 1993 Chemical Weapons Convention.

TECHNOLOGY

Technology can create faster, deadlier, and more accurate weapons, giving one army an advantage over another. Military technology is used in many areas, from uniform design to drones, fighter planes, and armed robotic vehicles.

But only rich countries can afford advanced technology weapons, as they are very expensive and also become out-of-date after a few years and have to be replaced by new technologies.

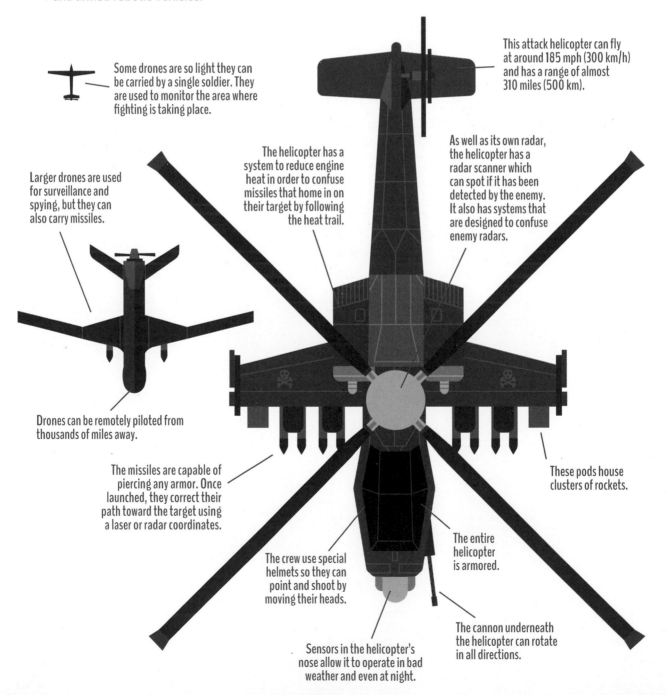

Some drones are so light they can be carried by a single soldier. They are used to monitor the area where fighting is taking place.

Larger drones are used for surveillance and spying, but they can also carry missiles.

Drones can be remotely piloted from thousands of miles away.

The missiles are capable of piercing any armor. Once launched, they correct their path toward the target using a laser or radar coordinates.

The helicopter has a system to reduce engine heat in order to confuse missiles that home in on their target by following the heat trail.

The crew use special helmets so they can point and shoot by moving their heads.

Sensors in the helicopter's nose allow it to operate in bad weather and even at night.

This attack helicopter can fly at around 185 mph (300 km/h) and has a range of almost 310 miles (500 km).

As well as its own radar, the helicopter has a radar scanner which can spot if it has been detected by the enemy. It also has systems that are designed to confuse enemy radars.

These pods house clusters of rockets.

The entire helicopter is armored.

The cannon underneath the helicopter can rotate in all directions.

In a war, each side has to convince their soldiers and allies that they have good reasons for fighting the enemy. Public opinion needs to see the enemy as the "bad guy" so that their own side is seen as "just," or morally right.

👁 SEE "THE JUST WAR," PAGE 16

The spreading of ideas or information to help a cause is called **propaganda.** In wars, it is used to justify the reasons for the conflict and to convince people that it can be won.

In the 1940s, the Second World War was fought on the **radio** and in **pamphlets**, **posters**, and **newspapers**. Today we use the **television** and **other media**, as well as channels that are harder to control like **social media**, **websites**, and **online videos**.

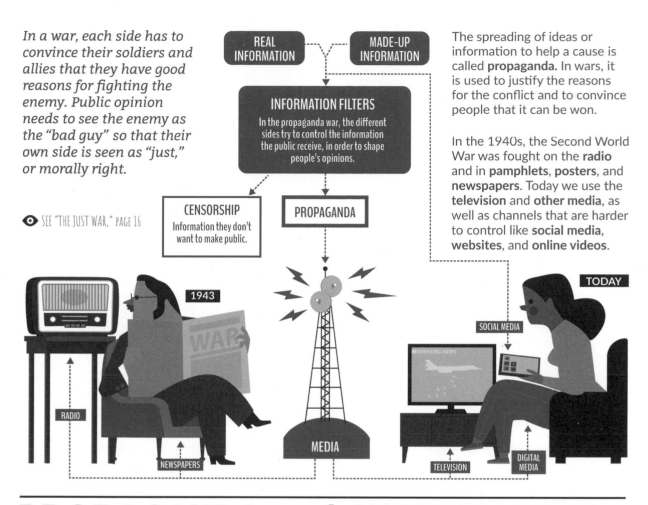

REAL INFORMATION

MADE-UP INFORMATION

INFORMATION FILTERS
In the propaganda war, the different sides try to control the information the public receive, in order to shape people's opinions.

CENSORSHIP
Information they don't want to make public.

PROPAGANDA

1943

WAR

RADIO

NEWSPAPERS

MEDIA

TODAY

SOCIAL MEDIA

BREAKING NEWS

TELEVISION

DIGITAL MEDIA

PROPAGANDA and CYBERWARFARE

The use of the Internet can go way beyond propaganda.

Cyberwarfare uses computer technology to strike the enemy, by destroying their IT systems with viruses or hacking into their systems to obtain secret information.

Imagine what would happen if an enemy managed to sabotage a country's IT network and shut down all its power plants or airports!

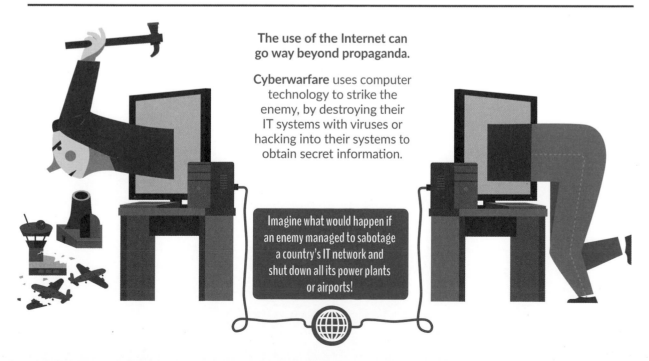

NEOLITHIC
Hunter-warrior

5TH CENTURY BCE
Persian army "Immortal"

2ND CENTURY CE
Roman legionary

7TH CENTURY
Tang Dynasty warrior

12TH CENTURY
Feudal soldier of the Kingdom of Aragon

15TH CENTURY
Italian knight

THE HISTORY OF WAR

Humans have always used violence. Early hunter-gatherer societies were probably already fighting "wars" to defend their territories or to steal precious resources from other groups.

As societies became more complex, so did warfare. Ancient Rome and the Han dynasty in China, for example, both commanded large armies which they used to conquer lands and fight other empires.

In places like Japan and medieval Europe, military power was held by the ruling nobles. Only they had enough money to pay for weapons, armor, and horses. Their armies fought against each other, even within the same kingdom.

Wars have always existed, but there have also always been people who believe that conflicts can be settled peacefully.

Great religious thinkers such as Confucius, Lao Tzu, and Jesus Christ all preached against violence.

In medieval Europe, religious buildings were places where it was forbidden to carry weapons and fight.

16TH CENTURY Landsknecht (German mercenary)

19TH CENTURY British marine

19TH CENTURY Prussian hussar

17TH CENTURY Spanish arquebusier of the Army of Flanders

19TH CENTURY Maasai warrior

20TH CENTURY French army officer

20TH CENTURY Cossack serving the Russian Tsar

The nobles lost military control when firearms were invented—their expensive armor was no use against bullets. From then on, battles were won by having a lot of foot soldiers on the battlefield.

Military technology allowed European countries to colonize other continents and impose their culture, religion, and languages on the conquered lands and people. Many of today's countries came about from this time of colonization.

As modern nations appeared, countries began to have permanent national armies paid for by the state. If war broke out, the army could call up part of the civilian population.

👁 SEE "WAR BETWEEN STATES," P. 20

*In the 16th century, Thomas More wrote **Utopia**, a book in which he imagines an equal society where violence does not exist.*

From the 18th century onward, Gottfried Leibniz and other philosophers started to think of ways of solving problems peacefully.

In the 19th century, socialism rejected war because it believed it only benefited the rich and powerful.

THE JUST WAR

Under what circumstances can war be a "just" (fair and right) option to settle conflict? Since ancient times, thinkers have questioned whether something as terrible as war, with all the death and suffering it brings, can ever be justified.

For example: if someone attacks you for no reason, do you have the right to defend yourself, or is it better to find someone to help you solve the problem?

And if you witness an attack, do you have a duty to intervene to try to calm things down?

The same is true for countries. If one country attacks another, should it be able to defend itself, and should the international community intervene to find a peaceful solution?

AGGRESSIVE COUNTRY   ATTACKED COUNTRY   INTERNATIONAL COMMUNITY

The problem is that things look different depending on who is looking at them.

What some people see as a just war may be seen as unjustified aggression by others.

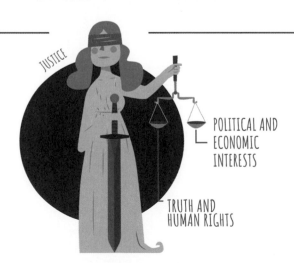

JUSTICE

POLITICAL AND ECONOMIC INTERESTS

TRUTH AND HUMAN RIGHTS

When war breaks out, the sides need to explain their reasons for fighting to justify the violence. This is why they start propaganda campaigns to prove that their cause is a just one. They often exaggerate or lie to defend their own interests.

👁 SEE "PROPAGANDA," PAGE 13

THE IDEA OF A JUST WAR HELPED LEAD TO INTERNATIONAL HUMANITARIAN LAW ▶▶

INTERNATIONAL HUMANITARIAN LAW
(IHL)

The laws and agreements of International Humanitarian Law (IHL) sit above and beyond the laws of individual countries. They exist to lessen the harm caused by war and to protect human rights.

Judges on **international institutions** (such as the court in The Hague in the Netherlands) are responsible for making sure that governments respect these laws. Those who do not respect IHL during a conflict are accused of committing **WAR CRIMES** or **CRIMES AGAINST HUMANITY**.

Governments sign international treaties and are responsible for making sure their armies respect them.

If governments notice that any of their soldiers are breaking IHL, those soldiers should be brought to trial and punished.

These laws govern what an army can and cannot do. For example, an army cannot invade another country, it cannot attack the civilian population, it must treat prisoners well, it cannot attack hospitals or medical units, it must respect historical or religious monuments, and it cannot use chemical or biological weapons.

 PROBLEMS

▸ Armies, with or without the agreement of their governments, do not always respect these laws.

▸ Irregular forces who do not belong to any government (most of the people fighting in today's conflicts) often don't respect IHL.

▸ Generally, it is very difficult to record and investigate when IHL has been broken in war zones.

INSURRECTION, UPRISING, REVOLT, RIOT, MUTINY, COUP, REBELLION...

REVOLUTION!

In a revolution, a large part of the population violently clashes with the political and economic system in order to overthrow it and put in place a new system.

Two of the most famous revolutions in history are the French Revolution (1789), which toppled the monarchy, and the Russian Revolution (1917), which overthrew the Tsar and imposed communism in Russia and many other nations.

COUP

A coup is when a particular group seizes political power quickly, violently, and normally without the support of most of the population. It is often officers from the country's own army who stage a coup to remove a civilian government.

REBELLION

In a rebellion, part of the population violently rises up against the government, either to overthrow it or to demand major changes in its policies. Unlike in a revolution, the people do not seek a big change in the social and economic system.

CIVIL WAR

This is a war within a country. In a civil war, people from the same place (even neighbors and families) who have different interests and ideas come into conflict with one another. Civil wars can come about when revolutions, coups, or rebellions fail to achieve their aims clearly and quickly.

GUERRILLA

In Spanish, this word means "small war." When Napoleon's troops invaded Spain in the early 19th century, some Spanish people rebelled against the French. They were small groups who could not fight a war against a large army, so instead they mounted quick surprise attacks and disappeared before the enemy could react. They were very hard to defeat because they were spread out, moved around a lot, and were able to blend in with the population.

Sometimes, the difference between guerrillas and terrorists is very small. For a government, guerrillas are terrorists, whereas the guerrillas themselves believe they are fighting a just war.

TERRORISM

Terrorism is when an armed group deliberately aims to create a state of terror among its enemies through attacking them at any time and in any place. The coverage of the attacks on television and other media helps to spread the fear.

Since the start of the 21st century, armed groups have tried to impose their religious views through the use of force. These groups are not from any particular country, but they have irregular forces based in several countries and they do not hesitate to use terrorism to attack their enemies wherever they are.

SPECIAL FORCES

These are elite groups of army soldiers who are sent to danger zones to carry out targeted attacks, using guerrilla techniques, infiltration, or sabotage.

See "Islamic State (ISIS)," page 39

WAR BETWEEN STATES

Modern countries, as we understand them today, appeared from the 17th century onward, especially in Europe. These "nation-states" are a form of political organization with land borders and a central government that passes laws, collects taxes, and has an army and police force.

During the 19th and 20th centuries, warfare between states was the most frequent type of armed conflict. It often involved conscripting many thousands of young men to go to war.

Wars like this have certain rules: countries break off their diplomatic relationship and formally declare war. In theory, their armies have to respect humanitarian laws on the battlefield.

THE WORLD WARS

The First World War and the Second World War took place in the 20th century. They were called "world wars" because they involved a large number of countries and were fought on nearly every continent.

These wars weren't just fought over land, but over ideas too. They were also the first wars that used modern technology (planes, tanks, chemical and nuclear weapons) on a massive scale, and the first wars to target huge attacks at the civilian population.

THE SECOND WORLD WAR

1939–1945 · In this conflict, the Allies (mainly Russia, the USA, France, and Britain, along with their colonies) fought against the Axis powers (mainly Germany, Italy, and Japan).

The war killed around 60 million people, many of them civilians, and caused destruction never before seen in history.

It ended in 1945 after Germany surrendered and the Allies dropped two nuclear bombs on the Japanese cities of Hiroshima and Nagasaki.

THE COLD WAR

After the Second World War, the two most powerful nations in the world were the **USA** and the **Soviet Union** (the name for Russia and several other countries). The two nations had different political and economic systems, and were prepared to do whatever it took to impose their system on the world.

To expand their **influence**, they got involved in wars and conflicts throughout the world, providing money and military aid to their allies. Wars such as the Korean War, the Vietnam War, and the Cuban revolution were all part of this confrontation between the USA and the Soviet Union.

Luckily there was **never a direct war** between these two military giants, because both states had developed **nuclear weapons** and the consequences would have been disastrous.

A **DEADLY** IMBALANCE

The two enemies had thousands of nuclear weapons. They knew that if one side launched an attack, the other side would respond, and so many nuclear bombs would be detonated that they would <u>destroy the entire planet</u>.

No one can win a war in which everyone dies, but both countries still carried on making nuclear weapons. They believed these acted as a "deterrent" that would discourage both sides from ever using them.

The Cold War ended with the breakup of the Soviet Union in the early 1990s.

MISSILES

A missile is basically a bomb with a propulsion system that allows it to be sent long distances.

The first country to develop missiles was Germany in the Second World War. Their V2 rockets were designed to bomb London and other cities without the need for aircraft. They were invisible to radar and could not be shot down by fighter planes, thanks to their supersonic speed.

The V2 rocket technology was later used to develop intercontinental missiles, as well as the rockets that would send people to the moon.

There are different kinds of missiles, which are designed to be fired from different places, travel different distances, and hit different kinds of targets. They range from a small missile fired by a soldier at a tank a few hundred feet away, to a missile fired from a boat at a military facility hundreds of miles away, to large intercontinental missiles that can cross oceans.

INTERCONTINENTAL BALLISTIC MISSILE

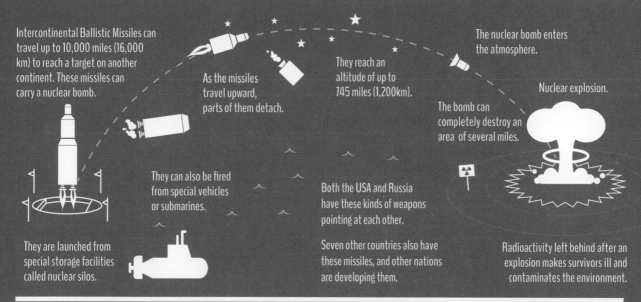

Intercontinental Ballistic Missiles can travel up to 10,000 miles (16,000 km) to reach a target on another continent. These missiles can carry a nuclear bomb.

As the missiles travel upward, parts of them detach.

They reach an altitude of up to 745 miles (1,200km).

The nuclear bomb enters the atmosphere.

Nuclear explosion.

The bomb can completely destroy an area of several miles.

They can also be fired from special vehicles or submarines.

Both the USA and Russia have these kinds of weapons pointing at each other.

Seven other countries also have these missiles, and other nations are developing them.

They are launched from special storage facilities called nuclear silos.

Radioactivity left behind after an explosion makes survivors ill and contaminates the environment.

The only time nuclear weapons have ever been used in war was in 1945, when bombs were dropped on the Japanese cities of Hiroshima and Nagasaki. They caused around 200,000 deaths and brought about the end of the Second World War.

Many nuclear tests have taken place in desert areas such as the Siberian tundra or small islands in the South Pacific. It is estimated that more than 2,000 nuclear devices have been exploded in the various military tests.

When the Cold War ended, the USA and Russia stopped making so many nuclear weapons. But both countries still have huge nuclear arsenals, and other countries such as India, France, and the United Kingdom also have nuclear weapons.

THERE ARE ENOUGH NUCLEAR WEAPONS TO DESTROY THE WHOLE PLANET.

MILITARY POWERS

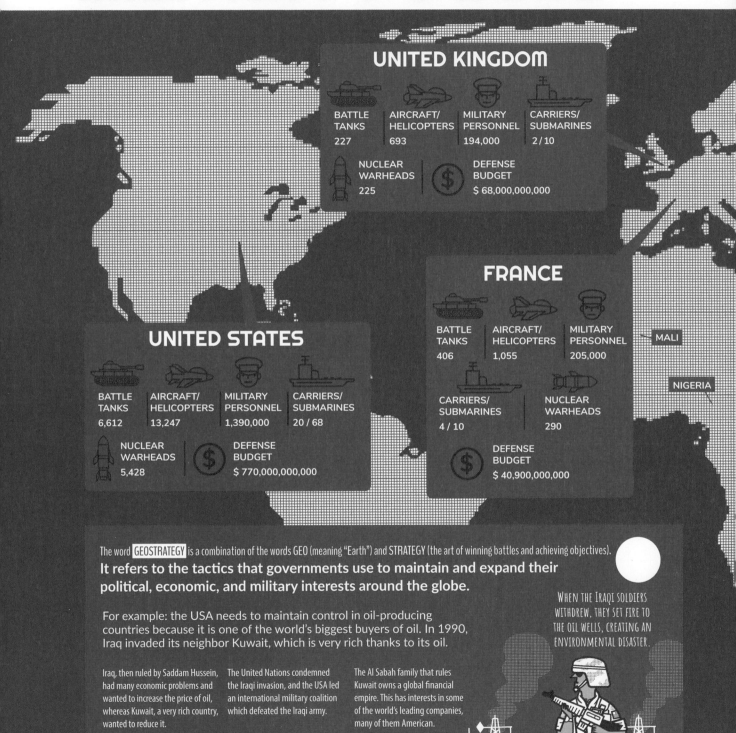

UNITED KINGDOM

BATTLE TANKS	AIRCRAFT/ HELICOPTERS	MILITARY PERSONNEL	CARRIERS/ SUBMARINES
227	693	194,000	2 / 10

NUCLEAR WARHEADS	DEFENSE BUDGET
225	$ 68,000,000,000

FRANCE

BATTLE TANKS	AIRCRAFT/ HELICOPTERS	MILITARY PERSONNEL
406	1,055	205,000

CARRIERS/ SUBMARINES	NUCLEAR WARHEADS
4 / 10	290

DEFENSE BUDGET
$ 40,900,000,000

UNITED STATES

BATTLE TANKS	AIRCRAFT/ HELICOPTERS	MILITARY PERSONNEL	CARRIERS/ SUBMARINES
6,612	13,247	1,390,000	20 / 68

NUCLEAR WARHEADS	DEFENSE BUDGET
5,428	$ 770,000,000,000

MALI

NIGERIA

The word GEOSTRATEGY is a combination of the words GEO (meaning "Earth") and STRATEGY (the art of winning battles and achieving objectives). **It refers to the tactics that governments use to maintain and expand their political, economic, and military interests around the globe.**

For example: the USA needs to maintain control in oil-producing countries because it is one of the world's biggest buyers of oil. In 1990, Iraq invaded its neighbor Kuwait, which is very rich thanks to its oil.

Iraq, then ruled by Saddam Hussein, had many economic problems and wanted to increase the price of oil, whereas Kuwait, a very rich country, wanted to reduce it.

The United Nations condemned the Iraqi invasion, and the USA led an international military coalition which defeated the Iraqi army.

The Al Sabah family that rules Kuwait owns a global financial empire. This has interests in some of the world's leading companies, many of them American.

WHEN THE IRAQI SOLDIERS WITHDREW, THEY SET FIRE TO THE OIL WELLS, CREATING AN ENVIRONMENTAL DISASTER.

US SOLDIER DURING THE IRAQ WAR

A military power is a state that has a large and very well-prepared army, including an air force and a navy, advanced military technology, and an arsenal of weapons of mass destruction. Which are today's military powers?

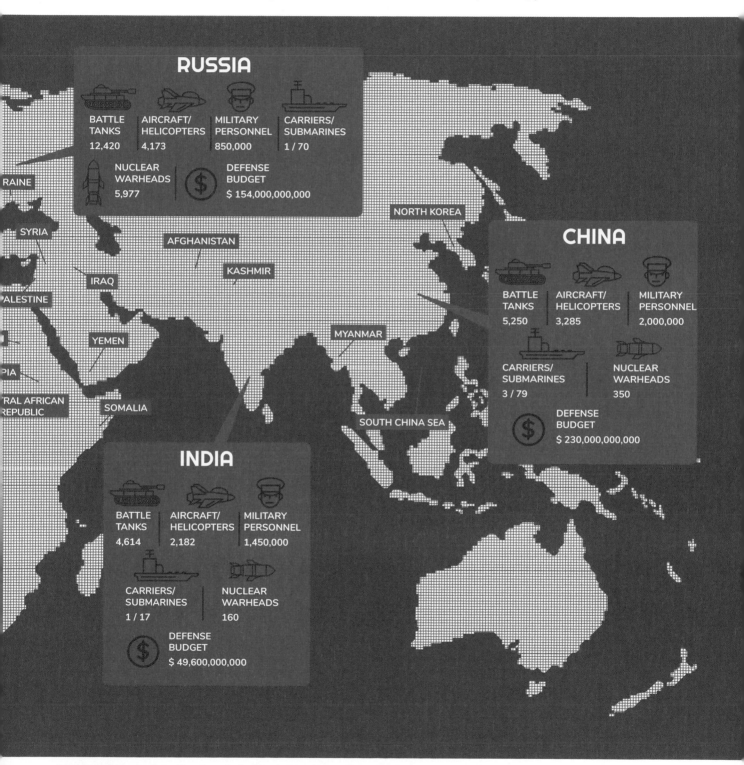

RUSSIA

BATTLE TANKS	AIRCRAFT/ HELICOPTERS	MILITARY PERSONNEL	CARRIERS/ SUBMARINES
12,420	4,173	850,000	1 / 70

NUCLEAR WARHEADS	DEFENSE BUDGET
5,977	$ 154,000,000,000

CHINA

BATTLE TANKS	AIRCRAFT/ HELICOPTERS	MILITARY PERSONNEL
5,250	3,285	2,000,000

CARRIERS/ SUBMARINES	NUCLEAR WARHEADS
3 / 79	350

DEFENSE BUDGET
$ 230,000,000,000

INDIA

BATTLE TANKS	AIRCRAFT/ HELICOPTERS	MILITARY PERSONNEL
4,614	2,182	1,450,000

CARRIERS/ SUBMARINES	NUCLEAR WARHEADS
1 / 17	160

DEFENSE BUDGET
$ 49,600,000,000

Map labels: RAINE, SYRIA, AFGHANISTAN, NORTH KOREA, KASHMIR, IRAQ, PALESTINE, YEMEN, MYANMAR, PIA, RAL AFRICAN REPUBLIC, SOMALIA, SOUTH CHINA SEA

Sources: globalfirepower.com/fas.org *Note:* the quantity of nuclear warheads in each country is approximate, as this information is usually secret.

AFGHANISTAN *These boxes show the places where there are conflicts involving one or more military powers.*

NATO and the WARSAW PACT

North Atlantic Treaty Organization—NATO

During the Cold War, the USA and its European allies made a **military pact**: if one of them was attacked, it would be considered an attack on all of them, and they would mount a military response together. This alliance was called the North Atlantic Treaty Organization, NATO.

Warsaw Pact

The Soviet Union and its allies did the same thing, by creating the Warsaw Pact.

The breakup of the Soviet Union in the 1990s ended the Warsaw Pact, but **NATO is still active**. It protects the USA and most European countries, including many that were once in the Warsaw Pact.

People's Liberation Army (China)

NATO is still the world's most powerful military alliance, mostly because it includes the **United States military**.

But there are other military powers capable of challenging it, in particular **Russia** (the heir to the Soviet Union's military power) and **China**.

NATO MEMBERS: Albania / Belgium / Bulgaria / Canada / Croatia / Czechia / Denmark / Estonia / France / Germany / Greece / Hungary / Iceland / Italy / Latvia / Lithuania / Luxembourg / Montenegro / Netherlands / North Macedonia / Norway / Poland / Portugal / Romania / Slovakia / Slovenia / Spain / Turkey / United Kingdom / USA

military bases

Some countries have military bases outside their own borders. These mean they can intervene quickly to defend the geostrategic interests of their governments.

After the Second World War, the USA created military bases all over the world. It still has around 800 bases in countries such as Spain, Germany, Japan, and South Korea.

Other countries have kept military bases in their former colonies. For example, France has bases in Africa, South America, and on islands in the Pacific and Indian oceans.

THE END OF WAR BETWEEN STATES?

Until Russia invaded Ukraine in 2022, it had been many years since there had been a lengthy war between two countries with powerful armies. Why?

In a global economy where companies operate in more than one country, countries no longer need to invade their neighbors to take their resources. Companies produce, buy, and sell all over the world, and wars are bad for business.

Diplomatic organizations such as the United Nations and the European Union help to prevent wars. The major powers and military alliances also avoid confrontation with each other due to the high cost of a conflict that could even lead to nuclear war.

The armies of smaller countries rarely dare to challenge major military and economic powers. They are more often involved in conflicts in their own country or region.

SO, HAVE WARS ENDED? THE ANSWER IS **NO**

There are still areas of tension between states, such as the border between North Korea and South Korea. Also, the armies of countries with less military and economic power continue to be involved in armed conflicts within and beyond their borders.

👁 SEE "NORTH KOREA," PAGE 34

What are today's wars like?

There are different types of armed conflict:

TYPES OF FIGHTERS

- National army against national army.
- National army against one or more armed groups.
- Different armed groups against each other.

BORDER WARS

- Within a country's borders. We call these "internal conflicts" or, if they are very big, a civil war.
- Between two opposing countries.
- In a regional conflict involving several countries.

FOREIGN INTERVENTION

- A foreign government or a group of foreigners give money and materials to one of the sides in the conflict.
- A national army or military coalition intervenes to help one of the sides.
- One or more armed groups intervene to help one of the sides.

INTERNATIONAL COMMUNITY

- Foreign forces intervene using military force to make sure humanitarian law is respected.
- The conflict is watched by the international community and the media.
- NGOs are on the ground.

Most armed conflicts today happen in countries which have a weak government and problems of poverty and inequality between people. They are fought by national armies and armed groups, and other countries and organizations may become involved.

MILITARY INTERVENTION

Military powers intervene in some armed conflicts to defend their geostrategic interests (see page 24). This intervention might just be providing their allies with weapons, military training, and money. Or it can be a more direct intervention of sending soldiers to fight on the ground.

If soldiers are sent, they rarely battle other armies. Instead, they fight guerrillas and paramilitaries. But, as the USA learned from the Vietnam War (fought in the 1960s to 1970s), it is very difficult to fight and win a conflict against guerrillas.

Asymmetric warfare

We talk about "asymmetric warfare" when a well-equipped regular army confronts irregular forces who have few resources, but who know the land well and are supported by part of the civilian population.

In a direct battle, the regular army would win with no problem. But in asymmetric warfare, the irregular forces don't engage with their enemy in direct battle. Instead, they hide in inaccessible areas or among people in local neighborhoods and carry out guerrilla actions and sabotage.

The regular army has to send in troops on foot to destroy the irregular forces and win. But a military occupation of a region lasts a long time, and is very dangerous and extremely expensive. That is why a regular army prefers to carry out targeted attacks from the air.

In such a situation it is very hard for anyone to win. The army does not control the region beyond its bases, and the irregular forces are unable to establish control over the territory without the risk of being bombed.

HOW DOES A WAR END?

Some armed conflicts can last for decades, but most end within a few years. It is very difficult for a society to keep military action going, and sooner or later the groups fighting have to surrender or find a way to end the conflict.

DEFEAT & SURRENDER

The classic way to end a war is with military victory (this is the aim of any armed group in a conflict). The loser has no choice but to withdraw, surrender, or both.

The winner then states the conditions for peace, and the loser has no choice but to accept them.

CEASEFIRE or TRUCE

Fighting is paused for a period of time, but the armies hold their positions.

ARMISTICE

Fighting stops, although the war is not formally over.

PEACE TREATY

Terms are agreed to bring a lasting end to the conflict.

PEACE and MEDIATION

When the opposing sides in a conflict don't seem to want to negotiate and find a way to end the fighting, international mediators can intervene. These are people who are neutral and whose aim it is to open peace talks. Getting the opposing sides to sit down around a table and talk is a major achievement in itself!

STAGES OF A PEACE PROCESS

Exploration →

Making contact with the opposing sides to understand their motives and explore their willingness to talk.

Negotiators →

Identifying the real decision-makers in the group.

Sincerity →

Finding out if the negotiators are sincere and really want to talk, or if it is just a strategy to gain time.

Rules →

Before talking starts, there needs to be a safe place for all the negotiators, and rules to follow.

Mediation

The negotiators have to accept that the mediator is neutral and is there to try to settle the dispute.

Conversations

Once these first steps are established, the rounds of negotiations can begin.
1 – At first, it is better to deal with any issues that are easy to reach agreement on.

2 – Based on these first agreements, more difficult issues can then be raised.
3 – In a negotiation, all parties have to give way a little on their demands, but in return they get something much more important: PEACE.

Peace agreements

There is usually a timetable laying out the steps to end the conflict: end of fighting, laying down weapons, agreeing land boundaries, exchange of prisoners, return of soldiers to civilian life, rebuilding programs, accepting neutral parties looking over the process, and setting up systems to make sure the peace agreements are respected.

CONSEQUENCES OF WAR

The years that follow the end of an armed conflict are called "post-war." This is a very difficult time, in which individuals and societies have to recover from the trauma and destruction of war.

■ Many fighters and civilians have lost their lives, causing trauma for their families and friends.

Many people are also left injured or disfigured.

In addition, people exposed to violence can suffer serious psychological problems.

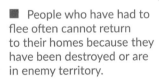

■ People who have had to flee often cannot return to their homes because they have been destroyed or are in enemy territory.

These people have lost their possessions and are likely to end up in displaced persons' camps in their own country or as refugees in another country.

Many seek political asylum in rich countries, but they don't always get it.

■ **Antipersonnel landmines** are buried underground, making them very difficult to detect and defuse.

In theory, these landmines are used against the enemy's army, but they are also used to make areas unlivable for civilians.

When mined areas are detected, the dangerous work of demining begins. But landmines are often in unexpected places and cause serious harm to anyone who steps on them: farmers, children, and animals.

■ Most factories are closed, public transport isn't running, and entire harvests have been lost, which means that food and other essentials are in short supply in the stores and markets.

■ **Infrastructure** such as roads, bridges, and power stations are damaged, but the state has no money to rebuild them.

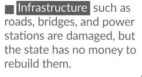

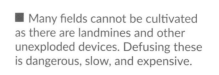

■ Many fields cannot be cultivated as there are landmines and other unexploded devices. Defusing these is dangerous, slow, and expensive.

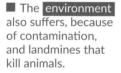

■ The **environment** also suffers, because of contamination, and landmines that kill animals.

■ The collapse of the economy and infrastructure make it difficult for businesses to start up again. People have no jobs and no money to buy things.

NORTH KOREA

Country: Democratic People's Republic of Korea, also called NORTH KOREA.

Government: Communist-style republic with a president. The president is called Kim Jong-un. <u>He inherited the presidency from his father</u>, Kim Jong-il.

History: During the Cold War there was an <u>armed conflict</u> on the Korean peninsula between <u>communists supported by China</u> and the <u>government supported by the USA</u>. In the end, a ceasefire was agreed, and the country was divided into two halves: North Korea and South Korea. North Korea is a military power with a personality cult around the figure of the president. Its only ally is China. It is also a very closed country that is difficult to enter and leave.

Problem: North Korea has been developing a nuclear program for a long time. It is suspected to have successfully developed nuclear warheads, as well as the ability to install them on an intercontinental ballistic missile (see page 23).

Since the Cold War, the USA has been an enemy of North Korea but an ally of South Korea and Japan, the two countries that feel the most threatened by North Korean military power.

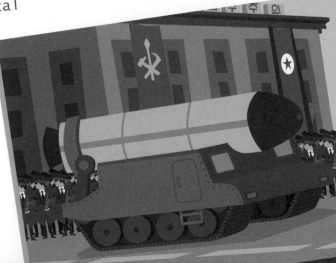

FILE
THE WAR IN
IN SYRIA

Atlantic Ocean

★ KYIV

★ PARIS   *IT TAKES THREE HOURS TO TRAVEL BY PLANE FROM PARIS TO SYRIA*

★ BUDAPEST

Caspian Sea

★ MADRID

Black Sea

★ ROME

Mediterranean Sea

★ ANKARA

RABAT

★ ALGIERS

★ TUNIS

★ ATHENS

SYRIA

Syria is a country on the coast of the Mediterranean Sea.

Most of its population lives in the area closest to the sea and around the Euphrates river.

Before the war, tourists came to the country to visit its historic cities such as Damascus (the capital), Aleppo, and the ruins of Palmyra.

Turkey

ALEPPO

Syria

BAGHDAD

HOMS

Lebanon

Israel

DAMASCUS

Iraq

Jordan

Saudi Arabia

The Alawites

The Syrian Arab Republic is a mainly Muslim country, although there are also communities of Christians and other religions.

Within the Muslim religion, Islam, there are two main branches: the Sunnis, who are the majority, and the Shias, who are a minority. The Alawites are a branch of the Shias.

Throughout history these branches of Islam have lived together but also fought among themselves.

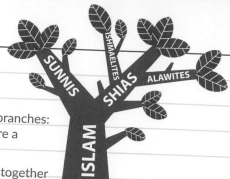

The Al-Assad family

Today's Syria gained independence from France in 1946. The Al-Assad family has ruled the country since 1971, first by Hafez al-Assad and then, after his death in 2000, by his son, Bashar al-Assad.

The Al-Assad family belongs to the country's Alawite minority. Important posts in the government, the Ba'ath Party, and the army are usually held by Alawites.

HAFEZ AL-ASSAD

BASHAR AL-ASSAD

IN SYRIA, THERE IS A STRONG PERSONALITY CULT AROUND THE PRESIDENT. THERE ARE PORTRAITS OF HIM EVERYWHERE AND HE CONSTANTLY APPEARS IN THE MEDIA.

The Ba'ath Party

The Ba'ath Party was founded in 1947 as a non-religious, socialist, Arab nationalist political party. It came to power in Syria and Iran in the 1960s.

In Syria, there is little difference between the Ba'ath Party and the government—most key posts are held by the party. Other political parties are allowed to exist, but only within the limits set by the government.

An ethnic patchwork

Most of the people in Syria are Arab Muslims, but there are also minorities such as Kurds, Druze, Yazidis, Armenians, Assyrians, and Turkmen. These minority groups have their own languages or religions, or sometimes both.

The Kurds are a people with their own language and culture who live in Syria, Turkey, Iraq, and Iran. Through history, they have often suffered aggression and repression in the states where they live.

Many people felt that the Syrian presidential system was not very democratic and was too harsh on the Sunni majority and on those who disagreed with the state.

How did the war start?

In 2011, some people began to demonstrate against the Al-Assad government.

The police violently repressed these protests, and the secret police increased their control over opponents of the government.

But this made many more people join the protests.

The conflict escalated and shots were fired at the demonstrators. They began to arm themselves.

Members of the army defected to join the demonstrators. But it soon became clear that the opponents of the government were not unified. Everyone had different ideas and aims, from those who wanted more democracy to those who wanted a stricter Islamic society. The different groups started fighting among themselves.

WHO IS FIGHTING THE SYRIAN WAR

 The war in Syria is a civil war, but it has an impact on all the neighboring countries and has led to the intervention of several military powers to help their different allies.

SITUATION
IN SYRIA
OCTOBER 2022

Al-Assad government

Al-Assad's government relies on the support of the country's national army and different militias and paramilitary groups.

In addition, there are different international actors helping the Syrian government:

IRAN Iran is a Shia country and usually helps Shias in the Middle East region. Since the start of the conflict, Iran has provided money and military advisers.

HEZBOLLAH This is a Shia political group and militia from Lebanon, a country that has also experienced very violent wars. Hezbollah is also supported by Iran.

RUSSIA Since the time of the Cold War, Russia has been an ally of the Al-Assad family.

Russia also has a naval base in the city of Latakia. This is the only naval base the Russians have in the Mediterranean Sea.

For this reason, Russia has intervened in the conflict to support Al-Assad's government with money, weapons, and mercenaries, and by sending Russian aircraft to bomb the government's enemies.

TURKEY

REBEL ZONES

ALEPPO

IDLIB

HAMA

TARTUS

HOMS

GOVERNMENT-CONTROLLED ZONE

MEDITERRANEAN SEA

LEBANON

DAMASCUS

REBEL ZONES

ISRAEL

JORDAN

Israel

In 1973, Israel occupied a strategic region called the Golan Heights.

Militias supported by Turkey

The Turkish army has intervened in the war by creating a "security zone" to protect the Turkmen minorities and to prevent the Syrian Kurd-controlled zones from joining together.

They want to stop the Syrian Kurds from becoming a country, because a Kurdish state might support the cause of Turkey's own Kurds (whom the Turkish army is fighting).

Kurds

The Kurds make up most of the Syrian Democratic Forces (SDF). They are well organized and control a large part of the country.

This group also relies on external support, particularly from the USA and its allies.

TURKEY

SDF-CONTROLLED KURDISH ZONE

Euphrates

ISIS ZONES

IRAQ

THE SOUTHERN BORDER IS STRAIGHT BECAUSE THE EUROPEAN POWERS DIVIDED UP THE AREA AFTER THE FIRST WORLD WAR

The **USA** *and its* **EUROPEAN ALLIES** *are supporting the Kurds and some rebel factions in their fight against the Islamic State (ISIS). They have provided financial, military, and tactical support, including bombing from aircraft and drones.*

As the Kurds and the rebel factions are enemies of the Al-Assad government, this intervention by the USA and its allies has led to tensions with Russia and Turkey (an important member of NATO).

Islamic State (ISIS)

This armed group wants to impose a very strict vision of Islam in an area between Syria and Iraq, which they have called the Caliphate.

Their brutal methods and terrorist acts have made them famous and feared, but ISIS now controls a fraction of the land it did a few years ago.

Rebel factions

There are several very different militias and armed groups that sometimes fight each other.

These range from army deserters to Sunni Muslims who want a strict Islamic society.

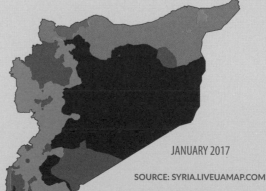

JANUARY 2017

SOURCE: SYRIA.LIVEUAMAP.COM

Consequences of the war

In Syria, there is a war of everyone against everyone. It is very hard to get information about what is happening on the ground. The groups do not respect humanitarian law, and it is difficult to discuss peace.

Nearly all of Syria is an arid desert, so much of the fighting has taken place in towns and cities where civilians live.

Bombing by air (including by foreign powers) has affected civilians and hospitals.

In 2013, Al-Assad's forces used chemical weapons against the civilian population. Other sides in the conflict are also suspected of using this kind of weapon.

■ DISPLACED PERSONS   ■ REFUGEES   ■ WOUNDED   ■ DEAD

A stream of refugees Millions of people have fled their homes due to the fighting. 6.7 million people have settled in other parts of Syria. Another 6.6 million people are living in other countries, many of them in refugee camps where conditions are harsh. Some have tried to reach Europe in search of a better future.

SOURCE: unhcr.org / syriahr.com

FILE
THE WAR IN
UKRAINE

On February 24th, 2022, Russian troops crossed the border into Ukraine, starting an open war between two states, a type of conflict rarely seen in Europe since the Second World War.

Україна
Ukraine

The country that we know today as Ukraine has for centuries been a borderland between Europe, the Russian Empire, and Asia. That is why it has suffered countless wars and many border changes over the centuries.

KEY POINTS

A SPOT OF HISTORY

Over the past few centuries, Ukraine has been divided between different powers, including Russia, Poland, and the Austro-Hungarian Empire. Ukraine tried to become independent around the time of the First World War and the Russian Revolution. But after much fighting between different groups, it instead became one of the republics of the Soviet Union. After the Soviet victory in the Second World War, territories such as the eastern part of Poland and Crimea became part of Ukraine. When the Soviet Union split up in 1991, Ukraine finally gained its independence, although Russia continued to have a lot of influence in the country.

A COUNTRY WITH TWO SOULS

Throughout history, there has been a strong Russian presence in Ukraine, and the Russian language is widely spoken, especially in eastern Ukraine.

The WESTERN part
Most of the population with Ukrainian ancestors is concentrated here.

It is the most mountainous area.

There is a strong Russian presence along the Black Sea coast.

The EASTERN part
Most of the population with Russian ancestors is concentrated here.

It is where the great steppes are.

It is also the richest part of Ukraine, with a lot of industry and agriculture.

- ■ RUSSIAN MAJORITY
- ■ MIXED REGIONS
- ■ UKRAINIAN MAJORITY

Many Ukrainians think that Ukraine as a country should distance itself from Russia and join the European Union (and NATO).

EUROPE ◄ ► RUSSIA

Many Russians and Ukrainians think that Ukraine and Russia have a shared history and that these ties should not be cut.

THE MAIDAN REVOLUTION

2013-14

In **2013, protests began** in Maidan Square in the capital city, Kyiv, with the protesters demanding closer ties with Europe. The protests, which had the support of Europe and the USA, led to terrible clashes between the police and protesters, but they succeeded in **overthrowing the government in 2014**. This was replaced by a new, pro-European government.

THE DONBAS CONFLICT

Donetsk

Luhansk

Sevastopol

Crimea

Many people did not welcome the new government, especially in **Donbas**, an area with a Russian-speaking majority in the east of the country. In **2014**, there was unrest in two regions of Donbas: **Donetsk** and **Luhansk**. People who wanted these two regions to be separate from Ukraine declared them to be independent republics. Since then, there has been fierce armed conflict in the region between the Donbas militias and the Ukrainian army and militias.

2014

Also in 2014, Russia annexed (took over) the **Crimean peninsula**. This region used to be the homeland of the Crimean Tatars, before it was conquered by the Russian Empire in 1783 and transferred to Ukraine in 1954. The Russian military base of Sevastopol (from where Russia controls the Black Sea) is in Crimea.

VLADIMIR PUTIN

Vladimir Putin is the **president of Russia**. He is an extreme nationalist who seeks to make Russia a **great power** again. Many of the former Warsaw Pact countries (see page 26) now have membership of the European Union or NATO (or both), and Putin sees this as a threat to Russia.

Since 2000

According to Putin, the aim of the 2022 military operation is to "de-Nazify" Ukraine, and to free Donetsk and Luhansk. However, Ukraine's government is not Nazi, and while some people want Donetsk and Luhansk to be part of Russia, others want it to remain part of Ukraine.

NATO'S EASTWARD EXPANSION

THE 2022 INVASION OF UKRAINE

In the first weeks of the military operations, Russian troops entered from Russia, Crimea, and Belarus in what appeared to be a rapid move to **overthrow the Ukrainian government.** The Russians gained control of parts of northern Ukraine, but faced much more resistance than expected and failed to enter Kyiv, the Ukrainian capital, or Kharkiv, the country's second biggest city.

After this failure, Putin's goals changed. His forces withdrew from the north and concentrated on **occupying the Donbas region and the Black Sea coast**, while continuing to shell targets across the country. In September 2022, Putin declared that the regions of **Luhansk, Donetsk, Zaporizhzhia, and Kherson had been annexed** and were now part of Russia.

The **prospects for peace in Ukraine are very bleak** at the moment. Both sides see the four annexed regions and Crimea as being part of their own territory and will not negotiate unless the other side accepts that. Until there is a change of leadership, or one side is defeated militarily, the countries will likely remain at war.

The Ukrainian army is a combination of regular army, militias, and self-defense groups. It can also count on the support of Western intelligence services and military advisers.

BELARUS

POLAND

Lviv

MAP KEY

■ Regions claimed by Russia

← Refugees leaving

← Initial Russian invasion

ROMANIA

MOLDAVIA

Transnistria

☢ THE NUCLEAR DANGER

Russia is a military power that took over the Soviet Union's nuclear arsenal. The fear of nuclear escalation is a barrier that prevents NATO intervening in the conflict. There is also a fear that Russia could use tactical nuclear weapons (a "small" nuclear bomb) on a Ukrainian target.

● 7.5 million REFUGEES

As in all wars, it is civilians who have nothing to do with the conflict that suffer the most. Over 7.5 million people have fled Ukraine, seeking refuge in European Union countries, especially those just over the border like Poland. As the European Union is Ukraine's ally, Ukrainian refugees have been able to cross the border without the legal problems faced by refugees from other conflicts.

Transnistria is a Russian-majority territory that rebelled in 1991 and declared its independence from Moldavia. No one has recognized it as a country, but Russia maintains troops in the region as "peace-keeping forces."

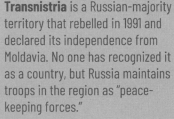

PORTABLE ANTI-TANK
ROCKET LAUNCHER

The powerful Russian army has the support of the Donbas militias, paramilitary groups, and mercenaries from different places, including Syria, Serbia, and Chechnya.

The European Union and the USA are Ukraine's allies. They have condemned the attack, imposed economic sanctions against Russia, and are sending a lot of military aid, which has been part of the reason for Ukraine's unexpected resistance.

In return, Russia put in place new conditions for buying its gas, before cutting off supplies. The European Union is heavily dependent on Russian gas.

RUSSIA

nobyl

★ KYIV

Kharkiv

Dnieper River

Luhansk

Dnipro

Zaporizhzhia

Kryvyi Rih

Donetsk

Mykolaiv

Mariupol

Kherson

Odesa

SEA OF AZOV

CRIMEA

BLACK SEA

Sevastopol

WAR CRIMES

There have been many air strikes on civilians and non-military targets. Civilians have also been killed by Russian forces on the ground.

REARMAMENT

Many European countries see the Russian military operation as a threat. They are increasing their military spending and moving closer to NATO. Sweden, Finland, and Ukraine have all applied for NATO membership.

PROPAGANDA, CENSORSHIP, AND CONTROL

As in all wars, governments try to control information. In Russia, it is dangerous to demonstrate against the war and the official government line. In the West, the Russian media has been banned.

GLOSSARY

allies
Two or more countries or groups working together to achieve a common goal. The group they form is called an **alliance** or **coalition**.

armed forces
The army, navy, and air force of a country.

asylum
Protection offered by a country to someone being persecuted in their own country.

ceasefire
An agreement between groups to stop fighting.

civilian
A person who isn't in the armed forces or police.

civil war
A war between different groups from the same country.

coalition
See *allies*

Cold War
The name given to the long period of tension between the United States and Russia and their allies from around 1947 to 1991. The two sides never directly fought each other.

colonize
To send people to settle in another land and take control of it. The land that has been colonized is called a **colony**. From the 15th century onward, several European countries, including Spain, Great Britain, and France, set up colonies around the world, even though the lands they colonized already had people living in them.

colonies
See *colonize*

communism
A type of government and economic system where everything, including land and property, is owned by the government, rather than individual people, and wealth is shared equally.

confrontation
A hostile situation or conflict between people, groups, or countries.

conscripting
Forcing people, by law, to join their country's armed forces.

de-Nazify
To remove Nazi ideas from a society. The Nazis were a nationalist, racist political group that ruled Germany from 1933 to 1945.

democracy
A form of government where people have a say in how their country is run, by voting to choose their leaders. If a government is **democratic**, this means it supports democracy.

diplomacy
The work of keeping good, peaceful relationships between countries. **Diplomats** are government officials who represent their country abroad and whose job is diplomacy.

displaced person
A person who has been forced to leave the place or country where they live, normally because of war.

economic sanctions
Actions taken by one country (or group of countries) to weaken another country, for example by limiting trade or banning travel.

ethnic group
A group of people who share the same background, such as language and history.

guerrilla
Someone fighting for a small, unofficial army, normally against whoever is ruling their country.

human rights
The basic rights and freedoms that belong to every person in the world, no matter their nationality, race, or culture.

humanitarian law
See *International Humanitarian Law (IHL)*

infiltration
A military tactic, where small groups of soldiers move through and into an enemy's territory without being detected.

International Humanitarian Law (IHL)
A set of rules intended to protect civilians and prisoners of war and limit suffering during a war.

irregular forces
Armed groups that are not part of a country's regular armed forces or police.

just war
The idea that some wars, fought in certain circumstances for "right" or moral reasons, are necessary and "just."

majority
When one group is bigger than another it is called the **majority**. The smaller group is called the **minority**.

mercenaries
Soldiers who fight for foreign countries or groups for money.

militia
A group of civilians who have been given weapons to fight with the armed forces.

minority
See *majority*

nationalist
Someone who strongly supports their own country, often also believing their country is better than others.

negotiate
Talking about an issue in order to try to reach an agreement.

neutral
Not taking either side in a disagreement.

non-governmental organizations (NGOs)
Organizations that work independently of government to support lots of different causes, from education and healthcare to women's rights and the environment.

paramilitary group
A group with weapons that isn't part of the armed forces or police.

personality cult
A term used to describe the excessive love and admiration felt by people for a political, religious, or other leader. The leader uses propaganda and the media to present themselves as great and heroic.

refugee
A person who has been forced to leave their country to escape persecution, war, or violence.

republic
A country that is ruled by an elected government, rather than a king or queen.

sabotage
To deliberately damage or destroy something.

secret police
A police force that works in secret against people who oppose the government.

socialism
A political and economic system in which people share all property and wealth evenly. Someone who believes in this is a **socialist**.

state
A nation or territory with a government and usually a definite territory.

surveillance
Watching a person or place to gather information.

treaty
An official agreement between different countries or groups.

United Nations (UN)
An international organization for promoting peace and cooperation around the world.

war crimes
Violent acts committed during a war that are against international law. See also *International Humanitarian Law (IHL)*

warhead
The tip of a missile that contains explosives.

First published 2023 in English by Button Books, an imprint of Guild of Master Craftsman Publications Ltd, Castle Place, 166 High Street, Lewes, East Sussex, BN7 1XU, UK. © Eduard Altarriba, 2018. English text © GMC Publications Ltd, 2023. ISBN: 978-1-78708-128-4. Distributed by Publishers Group West in the United States. All rights reserved. This translation of *What is War?* is published by arrangement with Asterisc Agents. The right of Eduard Altarriba to be identified as the author of this work has been asserted in accordance with the Copyright, Designs and Patents Act 1988, sections 77 and 78. No part of this publication may be reproduced, stored in a retrieval system, or transmitted in any form or by any means without the prior permission of the publisher and copyright owner. While every effort has been made to obtain permission from the copyright holders for all material used in this book, the publishers will be pleased to hear from anyone who has not been appropriately acknowledged and to make the correction in future reprints. The publishers and authors can accept no legal responsibility for any consequences arising from the application of information, advice, or instructions given in this publication. A catalog record for this book is available from the British Library. For GMC Publications, Publisher: Jonathan Bailey; Production Director: Jim Bulley; Senior Project Editor: Tom Kitch; Design Manager: Robin Shields; English Translation: Andrea Reece; Editor: Claire Saunders; Publishing Assistant: Charlotte Mockridge. Color origination by GMC Reprographics. Printed and bound in Malaysia.

Button Books

FSC
www.fsc.org
MIX
Paper | Supporting responsible forestry
FSC® C016973